D0190127

STRAIGHT TALK ON

Depression

STRAIGHT TALK ON

Depression

Overcoming Emotional Battles
with the
Power of God's Word!

JOYCE
MEYER

NEW YORK BOSTON NASHVILLE

Unless otherwise indicated, all Scripture quotations are taken from *The Amplified Bible* (AMP). *The Amplified Bible, Old Testament,* copyright © 1965, 1987 by Zondervan Corporation. *The Amplified New Testament,* copyright ©1954, 1958, 1987 by The Lockman Foundation. Used by permission.

Scripture quotations marked (NASB) are taken from the *New American Standard Bible®*, copyright © 1960, 1962, 1963, 1968, 1971, 1972, 1973, 1975, 1977 by the Lockman Foundation. Used by permission.

Scriptures marked KJV are taken from the *King James Version* of the Bible.

Originally published as *Help Me I'm Depressed.*

Warner Books Edition
Copyright © 1998 by Joyce Meyer
Life In The Word, Inc.
P.O. Box 655
Fenton, Missouri 63026
All rights reserved.

Warner Faith

Time Warner Book Group
1271 Avenue of the Americas, New York, NY 10020
Visit our Web site at www.twbookmark.com.

Warner Faith® and the Warner Faith logo are trademarks of Time Warner Book Group Inc.

Printed in the United States of America

First Warner Faith Edition: February 2003

10 9 8 7 6 5 4

ISBN: 0-446-69151-8 ISBN 978-0-446-69151-2

LCCN: 2002115540

Contents

————————⁓———————

CONTENTS

INTRODUCTION

———————⟿———————

*M*any people have bouts with depression. There are many underlying causes for depression and a variety of treatments offered to deal with it. Some are effective, but many are not. Some help temporarily, but can never permanently remove the torment of depression. The good news is that Jesus can heal depression and deliver us from it in the same way He can any other sickness or problem.

As I was preparing to speak on depression one time, I saw very clearly that God has given us His joy to fight depression. It was so clear that it seemed as though I was looking at a movie screen.

If you are a believer in Jesus Christ, the joy of the Lord is inside you. Many believers know this but don't have the slightest idea how to tap into it or release it. We need to experience what is ours as a result of our faith in Jesus Christ. *It is God's will for us to experience joy!*

Many people, including Spirit-filled Christians, not only have had bouts with depression, but major problems with it. I had problems with depression myself a long time ago. But, thank God, I learned I didn't have to allow the negative feeling of depression to rule me. I learned how to release the joy of the Lord in my life!

The message in this book is very simple, but very powerful. No matter what you have gone through in life or are going through now, if you are a believer in Jesus Christ, you have His joy inside you, and you can learn how to release it to win over depression!*

*If you do not have a personal relationship with the Lord Jesus Christ, the Source of this joy, see the prayer at the end of this book to learn how to receive Him into your life.

Part One

———❧———

RELEASING
GOD'S JOY

I

~

PHASES OF DEPRESSION

*I waited patiently and expectantly for the Lord;
and He inclined to me and heard my cry.*

*He drew me up out of a horrible pit [a pit of
tumult and of destruction], out of the miry clay
(froth and slime), and set my feet upon a rock,
steadying my steps and establishing my goings.*

Psalm 40:1,2

I

~

PHASES OF DEPRESSION

Depression in Webster's 1828 Dictionary is said to be "The act of pressing down . . . a low state." "A sinking of the spirits; dejection;" or "a state of sadness; want of courage . . . A low state of strength."[1]

Who Suffers From Depression?

People in all walks of life; professionals—doctors, lawyers, teachers; blue-collar workers—laborers; housewives, teenagers, small children, the elderly, singles, widows and widowers, and even ministers; can suffer from depression.

The Bible tells of kings and prophets who became depressed. King David, Jonah and Elijah are three good examples. (See Psalm 40:1,3; 55:4; Jonah 1 and 2; 1 Kings 19:5–8.)

I believe the reason so many people suffer from depression is that everyone on the face of the earth has to deal with disappointment. If we don't know how to properly deal with it, disappointment can lead to depression. From what I have observed, disappointment is the first phase of depression.

Dealing with Disappointment

All of us must face and deal with disappointment at different times. No person alive has everything happen in life the way they want in the way they expect.

When things don't prosper or succeed according to our plan, the first thing we feel is disappointment. This is normal. There is nothing wrong with feeling disappointed. But we must know what to do with that feeling, or it will move into something more serious.

In the world we cannot live without disappointment, but in Jesus we can always be given re-appointment!

In Philippians 3:13 we read a statement by the apostle Paul:

. . . but one thing I do [it is my one aspiration]:
forgetting what lies behind and straining forward
to what lies ahead.

Paul stated that one thing of most importance to
him was to let go of what lay behind and press toward
the things that were ahead! When we get disappointed,
then immediately get re-appointed, that's exactly what
we're doing. We're letting go of the causes for the disappointment and pressing toward what God has for us.
We get a new vision, plan, idea, a fresh outlook, a new
mindset, and we change our focus to that. WE DECIDE TO
GO ON!

Isaiah 43:18,19 says it like this:

Do not [earnestly] remember the former things;
neither consider the things of old. Behold, I am
doing a new thing! Now it springs forth; do you
not perceive and know it and will you not give
heed to it? I will even make a way in the
wilderness and rivers in the desert.

Isaiah 42:9 says:

Behold, the former things have come to pass, and
new things I now declare; before they spring
forth I tell you of them.

We see from these two Scriptures that God is willing
to do a new thing in our lives. He always has something
fresh, but we seem to want to hang on to the old. We hang
on in our thoughts and in our conversation. It seems that
some people want to talk about their disappointments in
life rather than their dreams and visions for the future.

God's "mercies" (KJV) are new every day. ". . . His
[tender] compassions fail not. They are new every morning . . ." (Lamentations 3:22,23). Every day is a brand
new start! We can let go of yesterday's disappointments
and give God a chance to do something wonderful for us
today.

You may be thinking, "Joyce, I've been disappointed
so many times, I'm afraid to hope." That place of hope is
exactly where the devil wants you to be! I know about that
place because I was there many years ago when Dave and I
married. I had been abused, abandoned and mistreated by
so many people that I was afraid to even hope things
would ever change.

But, through my study of God's Word, I came to realize that disappointment is a very unhappy place to live. I would rather hope all of my life and receive nothing, than to live perpetually in a feeling of disappointment.

Hoping doesn't cost anything, and it could pay off generously. Disappointment, however, is very expensive. It costs you your joy and your dreams of tomorrow.

We have a promise from God that those who place their hope in Him will never be disappointed or put to shame. (Romans 5:5.) I don't believe this means we will *never* experience disappointment. As I have already shared, no person can live in the world without being disappointed. I believe that verse means we won't have to *live* in disappointment. Keeping our hope in Jesus will eventually produce positive results.

Dashed Expectations

Dashed expectations lead to disappointment. We have many expectations in different areas every day. For example you may lie down expecting to get a good night's sleep, when in the middle of the night, the phone rings with a wrong number. Then after waking up, you can't go back to sleep for some reason. You toss and turn the rest of the night and get up feeling worn out the next morning.

We may expect the day to be sunny, but instead it rains. We may expect to get a raise at work and we don't.

We have expectations concerning other people. We don't expect good friends to gossip about us, but we find sometimes that they do. We expect our friends to understand us and meet our needs when we go to them, but they don't always do it. We expect things from ourselves we don't fulfill. Many times I have behaved in ways I, myself, did not expect!

I think we all expect more out of ourselves than we can give and frequently become disappointed with ourselves. We expect things from God that actually are not in His plans for us. Yes, our lives are filled with expectations, and some of them are dashed.

From that point when we are disappointed, it is up to us to decide what we will do—how we will respond. I have found that if I stay disappointed for too long, I will start to feel discouraged. Discouragement is a little bit deeper problem than disappointment.

Discouragement

Webster's 1828 Dictionary defines *discouraged* in part as, "disheartened, deprived of courage or confidence," and *discouragement* as "the act of deterring or dissuading from an undertaking; the act of depressing confidence," "that which depresses confidence and hope."[2] One meaning of *discourage* is "To try to prevent. . . ."[3]

Discouragement is the opposite of courage. When we are discouraged we have lost our courage. I believe God gives everyone who believes in Him courage, so naturally Satan tries to take it away. Remaining strong and courageous is one of the top rules for succeeding at anything.

In Joshua, Chapter 1, God told Joshua that He would cause Joshua to possess the land, but that he had to remain strong and very courageous. (v. 6.) I believe God was warning Joshua that the enemy would try to discourage him. We need to be educated on Satan's tactics and ready to resist each of them at the onset. (1 Peter 5:9.)

Proverbs 13:12 tells us, "Hope deferred makes the heart sick. . . ." When we become discouraged about something, we are also hopeless about it. We cannot be discouraged and hopeful at the same time. As soon as hope comes back in, discouragement has to leave. Sometimes when we are fighting to have a right attitude, we may vacillate between hope and discouragement. The Holy Spirit is leading us to be hopeful, and Satan is attacking us with discouragement.

At this point it is vital for the believer to get the victory in the Spirit realm. If he doesn't, his condition will worsen. Then he will begin moving into depression. A short period of discouragement may not have a devastating effect, but long-term discouragement can.

To get the victory and keep our attitude one of hope, we need to renew our mind to God's promises concerning our situation and stand in faith, believing God will do what His Word says He will do.

Levels of Depression

It is also important for the believer to get the victory early because a person who has become depressed can move into other levels or depths—there is depression, then there are the two deeper levels, despondency and despair. A mildly depressed person will not commit or consider suicide, but a person in despair will.

Mildly depressed people may feel sad and not want to talk or go out. They feel as though they just want to be left alone. Their thoughts are negative, and their attitude is sour.

The mildly depressed person may still have occasional rays of hope. It is that hope that will ultimately help pull the person out of depression.

A despondent person has all the similar symptoms of a depressed person, but the symptoms are deeper. He is "cast down" (in the terminology of Psalm 37:24; 42:5), dejected in mind, failing in spirit, has lost *all* courage and is sinking due to a loss of hope.

A person in despair, once again, has similar symptoms to someone who is depressed, but at a still deeper level than even the despondent individual. W. E. Vine's *Expository Dictionary of New Testament Words* translates the Greek word for *despair* in part as, "to be utterly without a way," "to be quite at a loss, without resource."[4]

Despair is distinct from despondency in that despair is marked by total loss of hope, whereas despondency is not. People who are despondent are hopeless, but haven't lost *all* hope. Despondency is followed by the abandonment of effort, or cessation of action; despair is sometimes connected with violent action, even rage.

People who take action to commit suicide, a violent act against oneself, are people who are in deep despair. Satan's tactic is to begin leading someone toward that point with dashed expectations or some other form of disappointment.

To avoid taking the path to despair, it is very important to deal with the first phases of depression at the onset!

2

THE POWER OF REJOICING

*. . . about midnight, as Paul and Silas were
praying and singing hymns of praise to God. . . .
Suddenly there was a great earthquake, so that the
very foundations of the prison were shaken; and at
once all the doors were opened and everyone's
shackles were unfastened.*

Acts 16:25,26

2

THE POWER OF REJOICING

Throughout the Bible, God instructs His people to be filled with joy and rejoice. For example, Philippians 4:4 says:

Rejoice in the Lord always [delight, gladden yourselves in Him]; again I say, Rejoice!

Any time the Lord tells us twice to do something—as Paul instructed the Philippians twice in this verse to rejoice—we need to pay careful attention to what He is saying.

The apostle Paul knew the power of rejoicing. When he and Silas were in the Philippian jail:

. . about midnight, as Paul and Silas were
praying and singing hymns of praise to God. . . .
Suddenly there was a great earthquake, so that
the very foundations of the prison were shaken;
and at once all the doors were opened and
everyone's shackles were unfastened.

Acts 16:25,26

The same power that opened the doors and broke the shackles of Paul and Silas and the others imprisoned with them is available to people who are imprisoned and shackled today with depression.

Many times people see or hear the word "rejoice" and think, "That sounds nice, but how do I do that?" They would like to rejoice but don't know how!

Paul and Silas, who had been beaten, thrown into prison and their feet put in stocks, rejoiced by simply singing praises to God. We don't often realize the "rejoicing" that can release so much power can be just as simple as smiling and laughing, having a good time and enjoying ourselves. And doing that in itself often makes the problem go away!

The time I was preparing to speak on depression when the Lord showed me something so clearly it was as if I were watching it on a movie screen, He said, "People come for all kinds of counseling because they're depressed. People take all kinds of medication because they're depressed. When people start getting depressed, if they would just smile, it would start to go away. Most people really truly do not understand that is how they're going to change their circumstances."

Change is often the result of a simple adjustment in how we respond in a given situation. The Lord was saying, "If they would just smile or sing a song to me, it would go away. If they would just laugh a little, depression couldn't stay on them. If they would immediately react this way just as soon as they *start* getting depressed, depression would leave."

The Scriptures clearly teach this, even though we might not have looked at the teaching on rejoicing in quite this way before!

Joy is simply a fruit of the Spirit.

But the fruit of the [Holy] Spirit [the work which His presence within accomplishes] is love, *joy* (gladness), peace, patience (an even temper, forbearance), kindness, goodness (benevolence), faithfulness,

Gentleness (meekness, humility), self-control (self-restraint, continence). Against such things there is no law [that can bring a charge].

Galatians 5:22,23

If you have a personal relationship with the Lord—if you are saved—the Holy Spirit dwells within you. (John 14:16,17; 1 Corinthians 12:3.) If joy is a fruit of the Spirit, and the Spirit is in you, joy is in you. You're not trying to *get* joy or manufacture it—it is already there, just as are the ability to love and the other fruit of the Spirit, because the Spirit is there.

It is very important to understand that we as believers are not to try to *get* joy; we *have* joy; *joy is in our spirit.* What we need to do is learn how to release it.

A Calm Delight

But none of these things move me; neither do I esteem my life dear to myself, if only I may finish my course *with joy* and the ministry which I have obtained from [which was entrusted to me by] the Lord Jesus, faithfully to attest to the good news (Gospel) of God's grace (His unmerited favor, spiritual blessing, and mercy).

Acts 20:24

According to Strong's concordance, the root of the Greek word translated "joy" in this verse means "cheerfulness, i.e. calm delight."[1] Meanings of one Hebrew word for "joy" are "to rejoice," "make glad" or "be joined."[2] Another Hebrew word translated "joy" can mean "to spin around."[3]

One of the meanings of "joy" in Nehemiah 8:10, ". . . for the joy of the LORD is your strength and stronghold," is "be joined." You can see that in order for the joy of the Lord to be your strength, you must be joined with God. Being joined with God causes joy in your life!

We can show forth the joy of the Lord in a way another of the meanings indicates by spinning around, in other words, with physical exuberance at times, but that doesn't mean we need to go around jumping up and down and twirling around in circles twenty-four hours a day!

Sometimes when people hear a message they recognize as truth, they want so much to apply it, they move into works—they try to make it happen in their own strength without allowing God to bring it to pass in their life as a result of prayer and God's power and timing. By saying sometimes we express God's joy by physical exuberance, I don't want to push anyone into doing this in the flesh.

When we don't feel joyful, we need to take some action to release joy before we start slipping into depression. Sometimes we must start in the flesh to rejoice whether we feel like it or not. It is like priming a pump by repeatedly moving the handle up and down until the pump kicks in and the water begins to flow.

I remember my grandparents had an old-time pump. Where they lived, folks didn't have running water in the kitchen back then. I can recall standing at the sink as a small child moving the pump handle up and down and sometimes feeling as though it would never take hold and start to supply water. It actually felt as if it was connected to nothing, and I was just pumping air.

But if I didn't give up, moving the handle up and down would soon become more difficult. That was a sign that water would start flowing shortly.

This is the way it is with joy. We have a well of water on the inside of our spirit. The pump handle to bring it up is physical exuberance—smiling, singing, laughing and so forth. At first the physical expressions may not seem to be doing any good. And after a while it even gets harder, but if we keep it up, soon we will get a "gusher" of joy.

I don't think *joyful* means that I am supposed to go around laughing hilariously all the time, spinning around, and jumping up and down with a plastic, frozen smile on my face. We need to use wisdom. I have had experiences with supposedly joy-filled Christians who actually hurt my feelings because they were insensitive.

I remember sharing something I was going through with a friend of mine. It was something that was really hurting me emotionally. Her response was a big smile and a loud, "Well, praise the Lord anyway!" I felt as if she had slapped me in the face.

If she had comforted me properly by showing understanding and concern, her ministry to me could have released real joy in my life. But her fleshly and phony reaction hurt me and made my situation worse.

When I first went to her, I was just sad. By the time she was finished with me, however, I was really depressed!

We always need to use wisdom. There may be times when we feel like spinning around in joy before the Lord. Maybe something really exciting has happened and we feel we can hardly contain it. But if we were in a restaurant or the grocery store, considering the feelings and reactions of those around us would be wise. We don't want to hurt our witness as Christians by doing things that make others think of us as emotional fanatics.

I've had occasions in a restaurant when I've told my family, "I feel like getting up on the top of this table and shouting, 'Praise the Lord!'"

There are times when an expression like that starts to come out of your inner man and you should give way to it. But if you're in a restaurant, grocery store, or some other public place, you might need to wait until you get in your car.

Although we can rejoice exuberantly at times, most of the time we rejoice by being glad and calmly happy. And, as the Lord showed me, that means smiling, or even simply living in a state of calm delight.

3

~⁀

SMILING IS SERIOUS BUSINESS!

. . . joy cometh in the morning.

Psalm 30:5 KJV

3

❧

SMILING IS SERIOUS BUSINESS!

I have a tendency to be a very serious, straight-faced individual. But I learned I also need to become very serious about smiling!

I was brought up in a bad situation and had a heaviness on my life. I didn't have a childhood—I was robbed of the joy of my youth. For as long as I can remember, I lived as if I were an adult because everything in my life was serious. I thought if I stayed serious, maybe I could stay alive. With this type of a background, you don't develop a bubbly, giggly kind of personality. I developed a serious attitude about me which can be misunderstood by people at times.

Once I told one of my assistants I needed to talk to her before she went home. She thought I was going to reprimand her for something. All I wanted was to talk to her about making preparations for an upcoming meeting. I had approached her so seriously, she felt she was in serious trouble!

I began seeking the Lord to find out how to be free from having such a seriousness about me. The Lord ministered to me that I need to express more of the joy that's in my heart. He knows it's there, but He wants it outside of us so that everyone can see it and benefit from it.

He ministered this to me while I was taking a shower one morning. I started to talk to Him, as I always do, when He spoke to my heart and said, "I wish you'd smile when you talk to Me."

My face didn't want to smile. At 6:00 A.M. it was stiff with sleep. But I started smiling! I felt kind of stupid smiling in my shower. I thought, "I'm glad no one can see me do this!"

Psalm 30:5 (KJV) tells us, ". . . joy cometh in the morning." When you open your eyes in the morning, joy is right there with you. You can't always feel joy until you activate it by purposely operating in it. Often the decision comes first, then feelings follow.

When the joy is obvious in your life, it rubs off on people. But when it's only inside you without being evident to others, you can create an atmosphere around you that is so serious, it brings a heaviness.

One night when Dave and I were talking, he said, "I feel there's almost too much seriousness in our home."

I started thinking about that. I asked the Lord, "God, there's nothing that I know of wrong in my life. I'm spending all my time praying, studying, loving You and taking care of my family. What is this Dave is sensing?"

The Lord ministered to me that we can have a serious commitment in our heart without being so serious on the outside about it that everybody else doesn't know how to react to us.

I began to realize that as a homemaker I could set the climate in our home. Joy is of light, and sorrow is of darkness. The two cannot dwell together. If I wanted my home full of light, I needed to "lighten up." I realized I needed to smile more at the people in my own home—not just give the children orders about their homework and chores, but smile or have a pleasant look on my face while giving those instructions. I needed to take the time to laugh with them and with Dave.

I believe our homes should be happy places. We should operate in the joy of the Lord. If a woman is joyful, her husband will be glad to come home. Everyone wants to go to a happy place. If he has a grouchy boss and complaining coworkers, he doesn't want to come home to more of the same.

Of course, the husband and children should also do their part to make the home a happy place. Joy is infectious. One person gets it, then another, and another and before you know it, everybody is happy!

Rejoicing Changes Your Circumstances

At times you reach a certain point in your walk with God in different areas and feel you're stuck there. You know there's much more, but you can sense something is blocking more from coming to you.

Dave and I reached that point in the area of prosperity. We had come from the point of having practically nothing to entering into a realm of at least not being concerned about how we were going to pay our bills. God was beginning to bless us. But I knew that God had so much more for us.

God wants to bless us so much. He wants us to live in nice homes, drive nice cars and be able to wear nice clothes. We are His children and He wants to take good care of us. Unbelievers should not have all the nice things while believers live on "barely-get-along" street.

There are certain things we do that bring prosperity because they set Bible principles into operation. When we give because we love the Lord and we want the gospel to go forth, we will receive. (Luke 6:38.) When we tithe, God rebukes the devourer for our sake. (Malachi 3:10,11.)

Dave and I were experiencing the kind of prosperity that results from giving and tithing, but because I sensed in my spirit it was time to go on into another level, I asked the Lord to show me what was blocking it. One of the things the Lord ministered to me was that joy is part of our receptacle to receive things from Him. Not showing outward joy in our life blocks prosperity from coming to us.

If the joy of the Lord is inside, but you don't smile and show forth the brightness of it, you'll look like a sourpuss. From a natural standpoint, how people see you has a great deal to do with their willingness toward you in many areas. People don't usually want to bless or help someone do something who looks like he might bite their head off because he looks so serious!

Every one of us knows how to smile. It's one of the greatest gifts God has given us. A smile makes people feel good, and people look so beautiful when they smile.

I would never have thought smiling was such a serious matter, but God spent several months trying to get this point across to me. Many times when God tries to tell us something and we don't heed it, we get ourselves in a mess before we realize how serious it is. Expressing joy through the calm delight of smiling will bring good things into your life besides showing forth the light of Jesus to others.

In the Bible the Lord told His people to rejoice when they faced their enemies. He told them to rejoice when they went into battle or when it looked as though they were going to die. He told them to rejoice no matter what—to sing, to praise with a loud voice. (2 Chronicles 20.)

When we are going through difficult times, we are to consider them wholly joyful. The *King James Version* says that we are to "count it *all* joy." (See James 1:1–5.)

God spoke to my heart, most people really, truly do not understand how expressing joy will change their circumstances. Operating in the joy of the Lord will chase off circumstances that are not godly because they are full of the devil. The devil can't stand God's joy, so if we operate in that joy, the devil and the circumstances will move out of the way.

Releasing the spirit of joy in the morning stops the circumstances Satan is setting up before they ever get started that day.

4

~∾)

Sing and Shout for Joy

Be glad in the Lord and rejoice, you [uncompromisingly] righteous [you who are upright and in right standing with Him]; shout for joy, all you upright in heart!

Psalm 32:11

4

~

SING AND SHOUT FOR JOY

Let the word [spoken by] Christ (the Messiah)
have its home [in your hearts and minds] and
dwell in you in [all its] richness, as you teach and
admonish and train one another in all insight and
intelligence and wisdom [in spiritual things, and
as you sing] psalms and hymns and spiritual
songs, making melody to God with [His] grace
in your hearts.

   And whatever you do [no matter what it is] in
word or deed, do everything in the name of the
Lord Jesus and in [dependence upon] His Person,
giving praise to God the Father through Him.

Colossians 3:16,17

Sing unto the Lord

We have already seen the power of joy and rejoicing in winning over depression.

In the above verse the apostle Paul tells us that one of the ways we are to express that joy and rejoicing in accordance with the Word of God is through the singing of psalms, hymns and spiritual songs.

In Ephesians 5:19,20 Paul goes on to instruct us: "Speak out to one another in psalms and hymns and spiritual songs, offering praise with voices [and instruments] and making melody with all your heart to the Lord, at all times and for everything giving thanks in the name of our Lord Jesus Christ to God the Father." The *King James Version* of Ephesians 5:19 says, "Speaking to yourselves in psalms and hymns and spiritual songs, singing and making melody in your heart to the Lord."

Let's have happy conversation with others and in speaking what the Word says to ourselves.

Sing and Shout Deliverance!

You are a hiding place for me; You, Lord, preserve
me from trouble, You surround me with songs
and shouts of deliverance. . . .

Psalm 32:7

Be glad in the Lord and rejoice, you [uncompro-
misingly] righteous [you who are upright and in
right standing with Him]; shout for joy, all you
upright in heart!

Psalm 32:11

In Psalm 5:11 David says to the Lord:

. . . let all those who take refuge and put their
trust in You rejoice; let them ever sing and shout
for joy, because You make a covering over them
and defend them; let those also who love Your
name be joyful in You and be in high spirits.

A few years ago a laundry product named "Shout" was
advertised on television with the slogan, "Shout out tough

stains!" That message prompted me to preach a message entitled, "Shout It Out!" In this message I encouraged believers that when Satan came around harassing and disturbing them, they should shout him out of their lives.

In my own life I used to be a screamer, but never a shouter. There is a difference. Finally the Lord came to me and said, "Joyce, either you will learn to start shouting or else you will end up screaming. Which do you want?"

So now when things start to go wrong in my life, instead of yelling and screaming at the top of my voice, I have learned to shout praise and glory to God. I "shout it out." You should try it—it beats screaming in anger and frustration.

Like David, I surround myself with singing and shouting. I have noticed that when I do that, I begin to feel better, because as David said, the singing and shouting act as a wall surrounding me on all sides.

But singing and shouting can also tear down walls and strongholds! We read in Joshua 6:20 an account of the Lord directing the people to shout and bring down a wall: "So the people shouted, and the trumpets were blown. When the people heard the sound of the trumpet, they raised a great shout, and [Jericho's] wall fell down in its place, so that the [Israelites] went up into the city, every man straight before him, and they took the city."

Now that does not mean that you and I are to go running all over town shouting at the top of our lungs wherever we may be! But at home there is nothing to prevent us from getting up in the morning with a song on our lips and praise in our mouth to the Lord God as a means to dispel depression.

I used to like the atmosphere to be as quiet as possible—especially in the mornings. I wanted to think! Actually, though, instead of thinking productively, I ended up worrying and reasoning excessively about things for which I could have never figured out a solution. What I needed to be doing was praying and trusting God about those things.

Within five or ten minutes after getting up in the morning, my husband would start singing or humming. He would have enjoyed listening to music, but I complained if he turned it on, telling him I wanted it quiet.

Since then, I have learned to listen to music as I start my day. During part of my prayer and fellowship time, I often listen to music.

God actually spoke very clearly to me in my heart on several occasions and told me that I did not listen to enough music. I had to develop a habit of doing it. At first, I did it in obedience. I was so used to quiet, I wanted it that way even though it wasn't always the best way to get my day started.

I don't mean to say that we don't need quiet because we do. God speaks in the still, quiet times, and they are precious. But I was out of balance. I needed to start my days happy, and the music helped me do that.

Even the great spiritual giant, David, had to battle with depression. We saw that David said to ever "sing and shout for joy." To overcome his downcast feelings and emotions, he used songs and shouts of deliverance. That's why so many of his psalms are songs of praise to God to be sung in the very midst of disturbing and unsettling situations.

When I am feeling down, I often go through the psalms and read them out loud, because I know that the promises in the Word of God will come to pass—as long as we don't just read it and confess it, but also do it, despite how we may feel at the time.

That is what Paul was referring to when he wrote to the Corinthians:

> For you are still [unspiritual, having the nature] of
> the flesh [under the control of ordinary impulses].
> For as long as [there are] envying and jealousy and
> wrangling and factions among you, are you not un-
> spiritual and of the flesh, behaving yourselves after
> a human standard and like mere (unchanged) men?
>   1 Corinthians 3:3

In other words, these people were not doing what the Word of God told them to do, but were doing what they *felt* like doing. Paul said that by so doing they were not operating by the Spirit of God, but by their own flesh. In Galatians 6:8 he warned that: ". . . he who sows to his own flesh (lower nature, sensuality) will from the flesh reap decay and ruin and destruction, but he who sows to the Spirit will from the Spirit reap eternal life."

That is why we must learn to do as David did and speak to our soul, our inner self; otherwise, it will take control over us and lead us to decay, ruin and destruction.

Wait Expectantly for God

Why are you cast down, O my inner self? And
why should you moan over me and be disquieted
within me? Hope in God and wait expectantly for
Him, for I shall yet praise Him, my Help and my
God.

Psalm 42:5

Does your inner man ever feel cast down? Sometimes
mine does. So did David's.

When he felt that way, when his soul was moaning
and disquieted within him, David put his hope in God and
waited expectantly for Him, praising Him as his Help and
his God.

This must have been an important issue with David
because in verse 11 of that same psalm he repeated almost
the same words: "Why are you cast down, O my inner
self? And why should you moan over me and be disquieted within me? Hope in God and wait expectantly for
Him, for I shall yet praise Him, Who is the help of my
countenance, and my God."

David knew that when he got down, his countenance
went down with him. That is why he talked to himself, his

soul (mind, will and emotions), and encouraged and strengthened himself in the Lord. (1 Samuel 30:6.)

When we find ourselves in that same depressed state—we should wait expectantly for the Lord, praise Him Who is our Help and our God, and encourage and strengthen ourselves in Him.

We who are righteous—in rightstanding with God— by believing in Jesus Christ, we who take refuge and put our trust in the Lord can sing and shout for joy! The Lord makes a covering over us and defends us. He fights our battles for us when we praise Him! (2 Chronicles 20:17,20,21.)

5

~

RESIST THE DEVIL
AT THE ONSET

*Withstand him; be firm in faith [against his
onset . . .].*

1 Peter 5:9

5

～

RESIST THE DEVIL
AT THE ONSET

There are many causes of depression—but only one source: Satan. He wants to keep us pressed down and feeling badly about ourselves so that we won't receive all that Jesus died to give us. One of his biggest tools to try to make us feel bad about ourselves is condemnation.

Condemnation can certainly be a cause of depression. Satan uses it to steal our joy. He knows the "joy of the Lord" is our "strength" against him. (Nehemiah 8:10.) Satan wants us weak and unable to do anything except put up with whatever he decides to throw on us.

People can also be depressed because of something that is wrong physically—sick people are frequently depressed; a chemical imbalance or being excessively tired and worn out can cause depression. If the body is depleted due to stress or lack of rest, the person may be restored simply by using wisdom and getting the needed rest and nutrition. If the depression is a medical depression, one that is caused from a chemical imbalance or other physical problems, obtaining proper physical help is prudent.

In other words playing music or singing and shouting will not fix people who are in a state of collapse due to overwork, depressed because their body isn't functioning properly with their hormones or body chemicals out of balance. We must pay attention to the physical need also.

Depression can result from physical, mental, emotional or spiritual causes. King David was depressed because he had unconfessed sin in his life. (See Psalm 51.) Jonah was depressed because he was running from the call of God and living in disobedience. (See Jonah 1 and 2.) Elijah was depressed because he was tired. First Kings 19:5–8 tells us that the angel of the Lord fed him two good meals and let him get some sleep.

We cannot always put all the causes of a problem in one box and pull out one right answer. But Jesus always is the right answer, and no matter what cause Satan has used to bring depression, Jesus will lead us to victory when we follow Him. He will show each of us what we need to do in order to live joy-filled lives.

No matter what the cause, as soon as we feel depression coming on, we need to resist it immediately and take whatever action the Lord leads us to take.

Don't Flirt with the Devil

Don't play around with depression. As soon as we start feeling disappointed, we must say to ourselves, "I had better do something about this before it gets worse." If we don't, we will ultimately get discouraged, then depressed. Jesus gave us "the garment of praise for the spirit of heaviness" to put on (Isaiah 61:3 kjv). If we don't use what He has given us, we will sink lower and lower into the pit of depression and could end up in real trouble.

When we know to do right and we don't do it, we are what I will call "flirting with the devil." In the world a man or woman might flirt with someone at the office, yet never move into a full-blown adulterous affair. But we cannot flirt with the devil like that. Once we open a door, he may get a foothold. Once he gets a foothold, he can obtain a stronghold. He is progressive and aggressive in his action against us, and we must be aggressive against him.

I remember when God revealed to me how wrong self-pity was. He told me that I could not be pitiful and powerful. I had lived in self-pity most of the time. At that time, I made a real commitment not to allow that negative emotion to rule my life any longer. When something didn't go my way, and I felt like feeling sorry for myself, I resisted the feeling right away. If I had let it go on, I would have moved deeper and deeper into it.

I recall one time thinking that I wanted to feel that way only for a while and then I would pull myself out of it. I was sitting in my prayer chair drinking my morning coffee. Dave had hurt my feelings so I wanted to feel sorry for myself. I knew I could not stay that way but was not ready to give it up just yet. The Lord showed me that by my not wanting to give up that feeling immediately, it was as if I wanted to have one cup of coffee with Mr. Pity. That may not sound too harmful, but it might be all the time the devil needs to get a stronghold that cannot be easily broken.

God covers us to a greater degree when we're ignorant and really don't know what we're doing. But once we know what is right and we willfully choose to do wrong, it puts us in a different arena. God still loves us and still wants to help us, but we have a greater degree of accountability. Knowledge gives us accountability.

Someone handed the following story to me during a conference where I was teaching on sin and how to handle it. It really brings across the point I am making.

A young girl was walking along a mountainous path. Making her way up the mountain it became very cold. While on her journey a snake approached her.

The snake said, "Please pick me up, I am cold."

The girl said, "I can't do that."

The snake said, "Oh, please make me warm."

She gave in and said, "You can hide inside my coat."

The snake coiled itself and became warm. The girl thought everything was O.K. Suddenly the snake bit her.

She dropped the snake and said, "I trusted you; why did you bite me?"

The snake said, "You knew what I was when you picked me up."

If we flirt with the devil, we will always get hurt. Refusing to put on the garment of praise because we don't feel like it or don't want to is dangerous. It opens a door for deeper problems that can cause serious consequences.

Resist Depression Immediately

Be well balanced (temperate, sober of mind), be vigilant and cautious at all times; for that enemy of yours, the devil, roams around like a lion roaring [in fierce hunger], seeking someone to seize upon and devour.

Withstand him; *be firm in faith [against his onset*—rooted, established, strong, immovable, and determined], knowing that the same (identical) sufferings are appointed to your brotherhood (the whole body of Christians) throughout the world.

1 Peter 5:8,9

Resisting Satan at his onset, will stop extended bouts of depression.

We resist the devil by submitting ourselves to God and by wielding the sword of the Spirit, which is His Word. (Ephesians 6:17.)

When Jesus was tempted three times by Satan in the wilderness, He did not get all wild and emotional. He simply said, "It is written . . . It is written . . . It is written. . . ." (Luke 4:4,8,10.) That is the way we are to resist Satan when he comes to tempt us into condemnation, depression or any other wrong thing he is trying to give us.

You and I must realize and remember that depression is not part of our inheritance in Jesus Christ. It is not part of God's will for His children. Anytime we feel anything that is not part of the will of God for us, that is when we need to begin to wield the sharp, two-edged sword of the Word. (Hebrews 4:12.)

The Bible has promised that if we will do that, if we will resist Satan firmly, at his onset, he will flee from us. (James 4:7; 1 Peter 5:8,9.)

The moment we begin to experience any feelings of depression brought on by condemnation or guilt or remorse or regret, we need to stand on the Word of God and refuse to allow those negative feelings to weigh upon us and depress us.

In Isaiah 61:1–3 we see that Jesus was anointed and sent by God to preach the gospel of good tidings to the poor in spirit, to bind up and heal the brokenhearted, to proclaim liberty to the captives, to open the prison doors and the eyes of those who are bound, and to grant consolation and joy to those who mourn—to give them an ornament of beauty instead of ashes, the oil of joy instead of mourning, and a garment of praise instead of a heavy, burdened, and failing spirit.

In Christ There Is No Condemnation

Therefore, [there is] now no condemnation (no adjudging guilty of wrong) for those who are in Christ Jesus, who live [and] walk not after the dictates of the flesh, but after the dictates of the Spirit.

Romans 8:1

According to this Scripture, we who are in Christ Jesus are no longer condemned, no longer judged guilty or wrong. Yet so often we judge and condemn ourselves.

In my own case, until I learned and understood the Word of God, I lived a large part of my life feeling guilty. If someone had asked me what I felt guilty about, I could not have answered. All I knew was that there was a vague feeling of guilt that followed me around all the time. Fortunately, when I came to better understand the Word of the Lord, I was able to overcome that nagging feeling.

But not too long ago I went through a short period in which I felt that old sense of guilt. It took me a couple of days to recognize what was happening, because I had not had a problem like that for a long time.

From that experience, God gave me a real revelation about walking free from guilt and condemnation. He showed me that you and I must not only receive forgiveness from Him, we must also forgive ourselves. We must stop beating ourselves over the head for something that He has forgiven and forgotten. (Jeremiah 31:34; Acts 10:15.)

That does not mean that we are now perfect or incapable of error. It just means that we can go on with our lives without being weighed down with a constant burden of guilt and condemnation for what is in the past.

As long as we are doing the best we can, we truly repent for our sins and our heart is right before God, we can stay out from under the burden of guilt and condemnation.

God not only looks at what we do; He looks at our heart. He knows that if our heart is right, then our actions will eventually come into line with our heart.

During the period I was going through feelings of guilt and condemnation, everything I did bothered me. I felt guilty and condemned for every little mistake I made. Finally I told my husband, "Dave, I believe I am being attacked by a spirit of condemnation."

That happens from time to time to each of us. We may wake up one day and for no apparent reason suddenly feel that we have done something wrong. If that feeling continues, we may begin to ask ourselves, "What's wrong with me?"

That is when we need to exercise the spiritual authority over the demonic forces that has been given to us in the name and by the blood of Jesus. That is when we need to use the Word of God to overcome the powers that would try to rob us of our peace and joy in the Lord.

God Wants to Help You

Some people, born with more of an "up" personality, don't have problems with depression. But there are many others; including born-again, Spirit-filled Christians; who suffer from it regularly.

If you are suffering from depression, know that God loves you more than you can imagine and cares about your problem. He doesn't want you to have to suffer with it anymore. But if you do become depressed again, which you may, you don't need to become guilty or feel condemned over it.

I apply in my life the principles in this book on a regular basis. If I didn't, I could end up depressed four to five days a week.

I believe it is nearly impossible to get depressed if the mind is kept under strict control. That is why we are told in Isaiah 26:3 that God will guard and keep us in perfect and constant peace—if we will keep our mind stayed on Him.

If we are in perfect and constant peace, then we will not be depressed. Ninety-nine and nine-tenths percent of our problems begin in our mind.

> You will guard him and keep him in perfect and
> constant peace whose mind [both its inclination
> and its character] is stayed on You, because he
> commits himself to You, leans on You, and hopes
> confidently in You.
> So trust in the Lord (commit yourself to
> Him, lean on Him, hope confidently in Him)
> forever; for the Lord God is an everlasting Rock
> [the Rock of Ages].
>
> Isaiah 26:3,4

6

REJECTION, FAILURE AND UNFAIR COMPARISONS

Although my father and my mother have forsaken me, yet the Lord will take me up [adopt me as His child].

Psalm 27:10

6

⟳

REJECTION, FAILURE AND UNFAIR COMPARISONS

Rejection causes depression. To be rejected means to be thrown away as having no value or as being unwanted. We were created for acceptance, not rejection. The emotional pain of rejection is one of the deepest kinds known. Especially if the rejection comes from someone we love or expect to love us, like parents or a spouse.

I once knew a woman who was deeply depressed most of the time even though she was a Christian and had a lovely family. Her depression seemed to stem from the fact that she was adopted. She said she had a deep feeling that something was wrong with her and because of that she was unwanted. She expressed it as a big hole in her heart that nothing seemed to fill up.

She desperately needed to RECEIVE the love of God. I emphasize "receive" because many people mentally assent that God loves them, even saying it, but it is not a reality in their life.

Psalm 27:10 says,

Although my father and my mother have forsaken me, yet the Lord will take me up [adopt me as His child].

God had accepted her and loved her very much, but she was ruining her life trying to get something that she would never have—the love of her natural parents.

This longing made her feel depressed. Satan had taken advantage of her emotions through this open door early in her life. Depression had become a habitual pattern. She was so accustomed to feeling that way, just floating along in those same old negative feelings was easy.

When we are saved by Jesus from our sins, our emotions are not saved. We may still "feel" many negative things. But at that moment or time of salvation—the time when we accept Jesus Christ as Our Lord and Savior and believe on Him—we do receive the fruit of the Holy Spirit.

One of the fruits is the fruit of self-control. (Galatians 5:22,23 NASB.) It is this fruit that will save us from all these negative emotions. We learn what God's Word says about emotions, then we begin with the help of the Holy Spirit to control the negative ones and not give them expression through our bodies, which now belong to Jesus Christ.

This young woman, although a Christian, was living in the carnal realm. She was following ordinary impulses. She needed to begin getting her worth and value out of the fact that Jesus loved her enough to die for her and stop feeling that she was unloved and valueless because her parents did not keep her. She eventually got the victory, but it was a long, hard battle.

If you have been depressed, it might be due to a root of rejection in your life. Overcoming rejection is certainly not easy, but we can overcome it through the love of Jesus Christ.

In Ephesians 3:18,19 Paul prayed for the church that they would know "the breadth and length and height and depth" of the love that God had for them and that they would experience it for themselves. He said this experience far surpasses mere knowledge.

Watch for all the ways that God shows His love for you, and it will overcome the rejection you may have experienced from other people.

Here is an example:

While I was working on this chapter of the book, I received a phone call letting me know that a certain very well-known pastor had called. He has many wonderful meetings in his church, but had never wanted to make his building available for other ministries to use. This pastor had absolutely never allowed ministries like mine to use his church auditorium to hold a conference, but he called stating that God had placed on his heart to let us use it!

We had outgrown the church we had been using previously and were at the point of needing to quit using that building because we couldn't fit in it. The only option we saw was to rent a civic center which can sometimes be very costly and usually involves a lot of red tape.

So often we just let things which happen like that go by without realizing they are of God Who is showing His love for us. Every time God gives us favor, He is showing us that He loves us. There are many, many ways He shows

His love for us all the time; we simply need to begin watching for it. Having a deep revelation concerning God's love for us will keep us from depression.

When people reject us, Jesus takes it personally. Luke 10:16 states:

> He who hears and heeds you [disciples] hears and heeds Me; and he who slights and rejects you slights and rejects Me; and he who slights and rejects Me slights and rejects Him Who sent Me.

Think about it—even if someone slights us, Jesus takes it personally. It is an evil thing for one person to reject another. James 2:8,9 teaches us that Love is the new law and that ". . . if you show servile regard (prejudice, favoritism) for people, you commit sin and are rebuked and convicted by the Law as violators and offenders." We are breaking that law of love.

Although rejection is an evil thing, we don't have to allow the evil to control our emotions and depress us. Romans 12:21 states, "Do not let yourself be overcome by evil, but overcome (master) evil with good."

Putting a smile on our face and being joyful on purpose is a good thing, and it will overcome the evil of rejection and the result of depression.

Failure

We are programmed by society to believe that winning is everything and that success means living without failure. I personally believe that failure is part of true success.

What I mean is this: Everyone on their way up has a few things to learn. One of those things is humility. People are not just automatically humble, we all deal with a generous portion of pride. A few rounds of failure works humility into our character very quickly!

Peter was a powerful apostle. We might say he was a success and made it to the top—He obeyed the Lord and allowed Him to accomplish great things for the kingdom of God through Peter. But Peter failed miserably when he denied three times that he even knew Jesus.

Paul also was a mighty man of God, yet he stated that he had weaknesses. David was a tremendous king and psalmist and prophet, but he failed in that he committed adultery with Bathsheba and arranged to have her husband Uriah killed.

I have a very successful ministry now, but I sure made a lot of mistakes and failed at various times on my way to the position I now have. I thought I was hearing from God at times, then discovered I wasn't. I stepped out in things that were not God's will for me and had to back down, sometimes very embarrassed. I failed to always treat people with the love and mercy that Jesus would have.

My failures disappointed me and sometimes discouraged and even depressed me. As a matter of fact, that was my normal response until I realized that God was using my weaknesses, turning them to the good, to develop my character and make me a better person.

No person has truly failed until they stop trying. I keep the outlook that Satan may knock me down, but he is not going to knock me out. Failing at something is quite different than being a failure. We must learn to separate our "who" and our "do." I may "do" something that I fail at, but "I" am not a failure. I am a child of God who is still being changed into His image, from glory to glory. (2 Corinthians 3:18.)

It is really not failure that causes depression; it is our attitude toward it. If we believe God is greater than our failures, then they have no power over us! Our weaknesses are an opportunity for Him to show His strength.

Romans 5:20 (KJV) says, ". . . where sin abounded, grace did much more abound." How can anyone fail with a system like that set in motion on their behalf?

Don't be depressed over weaknesses and failures. Rejoice in knowing that because of Jesus, you don't have to stay that way. People without the Lord in their lives only have depression to go to when they fail, but we can go to Jesus. That should make us happy, not sad!

Remember that you are no surprise to God. He knew what He was getting when He chose you, the same as He knew what He was getting when He chose me. Ephesians 1:4 says, "He chose us [actually picked us out for Himself as His own] in Christ before the foundation of the world." He already knew every weakness, every flaw, every time we would ever fail, and He still said, "I want you." Ephesians 1:5 states that He foreordained us to be adopted as His own children.

I think I'll be happy—God is my daddy! With God on our side things are bound to work out all right in the end. So let's rejoice now and not waste all that time being sad.

Unfair Comparisons

Comparing our lives with other people's lives frequently causes depression. We can look at other people and wonder why we don't look like they look, know what they know, own what they own or do what they do. But, it's interesting to note that Satan never points out what they don't have, only what they *do* have that *we* don't have.

Others may have some things that we don't, but we also have some things that they don't have. We must believe that God equipped each of us with just what we need to fulfill His call on our lives. If I don't have it, I must not need it, or it just isn't time yet for me to have it.

I spent many unhappy, depressed days comparing myself with other people. Why couldn't I cast my care like Dave? Why couldn't I be sweet, merciful and submissive like my pastor's wife? Why couldn't I sew like my neighbor? Why can't I have a faster working metabolism so I can eat more and not gain weight? Why? Why? Why?

God never answered me except with the same answer that he gave Peter when he compared himself with John. In John 21:18–22 Jesus had told Peter that Peter was going to enter a time of suffering. He was speaking of the kind of death Peter would die and thereby glorify God.

Peter's initial response was to ask what was going to happen to John. Jesus promptly said, "If I want him to stay (survive, live) till I come, what is that to you? [What concern is it of yours?] You follow Me!" (v. 22).

It sounds to me as if Jesus was politely telling Peter to mind his own business, not compare himself with John. The Lord has an individual plan for each of us, and often we can't understand what He is doing or why He is doing it.

We look at other people as the standard for what should happen to us, but they cannot be the standard because God sets a new standard with each person. That we all have a different set of fingerprints, is proof enough we are not to compete with one another and live in unfair comparisons.

It is unfair to compare ourselves with others. It is unfair to us, to them and to God. It pressures relationships and says to God, "I want to limit You to this and nothing else." What if God ends up giving you something far greater than anyone you know?

We would be satisfied with what we see other people have, but God can go beyond that for the person who will trust Him. Galatians 5:26 teaches us not to be "envying" and "jealous" of one another, "competitive," in that regard.

Proverbs 14:30 says, ". . . envy, jealousy, and wrath are like rottenness of the bones." Depression feels just like that—"rottenness of the bones." Everything feels as if it has caved in.

Galatians 6:4 tells us to do "something commendable [in itself alone] without [resorting to] boastful comparison with his neighbor." In other words our goal should be to be "the very best me I can be," to just do what we believe we are supposed to do without seeking to do something "greater than" someone else so we can feel better about ourselves.

When our value as an individual is firmly rooted in Christ, we are free from the agony of comparisons and competition. That kind of freedom releases joy. Depression is the result of looking at what we don't have and can't do. Joy is the result of being thankful for every little thing we have and counting ourselves blessed just to be alive and to know Jesus as our Lord.

Depression Begets Depression

Our associations are very important for we can become like whoever we are around. Daniel was a great man of integrity and excellence, but I noticed that his friends were the same way. Daniel would not compromise, but neither would Shadrach, Meshach, and Abednego.

A depressed, gloomy, negative person is very unpleasant to be around. If those around the person are not careful, they will find themselves starting to feel the same way the depressed person does.

If you have to be around someone regularly that is depressed, keep yourself covered by faith with the blood of Jesus for protection against the spirit of depression. Be sure you are more aggressive against depression than it is against you.

Psalm 1:1 tells us not to sit inactive in the pathway of sinners. I firmly believe in trying to help people, and this would include depressed people, but sometimes they don't want help, they just want to be depressed.

I have dealt with individuals who were so negative, no matter what kind of good things I tried to point out, they would always come back with something sour and negative. I was that way myself for a good number of years, and it would actually make me mad when someone would try to cheer me up.

I can well remember how Dave would persist in being happy no matter how gloomy I was. His joy actually made me angry!

Depressed people want others to be depressed. Joy irritates them. Actually it irritates the evil spirit that is oppressing them. I am not saying that people who are depressed are all possessed by the devil. I am saying that depression is the result of an evil spirit oppressing us.

We know that all wicked and evil things come from Satan and his demons, so let's face it for what it is and not be offended.

If you are someone who is being attacked with bouts of depression and you sincerely want to overcome it, one of the things you can do is make sure you spend time with happy people. Dave's joy irritated me in my depressed days, but his stability and joy also made me hungry for what he had.

I learned from being around him how to handle situations. I saw how differently he handled things from the way I handled them, and I began to realize that his joy was not due to his never having any challenges in life—it was due to how he handled them—his attitude toward them.

Spirits and anointings are transferable. That is why we lay hands on people which is a biblical doctrine. Seventy men were chosen to help Moses in the ministry to which God called him. First God said to bring them to the tent of meeting and let them stand there with him, then He would come and take of the Spirit upon Moses and put it upon them.

First they had to just get around Moses—just stand there with him—and God would see to it that the Spirit on him, got on them. Powerful principle isn't it!

I needed a lot of change in my personality. One of the things I needed most was stability in my moods. God understood why I was the way I was. There were many things that had happened to me over the years that developed the moodiness in my emotional nature. But He also arranged for my healing. He surrounded me in my personal life with people who were extremely stable.

My husband was one, and so were a couple who have lived with Dave and me for eleven years and taken care of our home and ministry when we are traveling. Paul and Roxane are both very stable.

All three of these people are people I talk with almost daily, eat most of my meals with, watch movies with, shop with, go to church with, talk to, make plans with, and so on. I was so surrounded by happy, stable people that I looked like a big spot or blemish until I changed. Their joy and stability convicted me and I am glad for it. That is what happy, joy-filled, stable people can do for you.

So if you're battling depression, remember that your associations are very important. Don't associate with depressed people if you need to get over depression yourself!

The last thing we need when we are experiencing bouts of depression is to get together with other discouraged, depressed people and talk about all of our problems. We need to laugh, sing, rejoice, shout occasionally and think about happy things.

7

❧

LISTEN TO WHAT
GOD SAYS ABOUT YOU

*To the praise of the glory of his grace, wherein he
hath made us accepted in the beloved.*

Ephesians 1:6 KJV

7

꩜

LISTEN TO WHAT
GOD SAYS ABOUT YOU

God does not want us to feel frustrated and condemned. He wants us to realize that we are pleasing to Him just as we are.

The devil keeps trying to tell us what we are not, but God keeps trying to tell us what we are—His beloved children who are well-pleasing to Him.

God never reminds us of how far we have fallen, He always reminds us of how far we have risen. He reminds us of how much we have overcome, how well we are doing, how precious we are in His sight, how much He loves us.

The devil tells us we cannot possibly be acceptable to God because we are not perfect, but God tells us that we are accepted in the Beloved because of what He has already done for us. (Ephesians 1:6 KJV.)

God wants us to know that His hand is upon us, that His angels are watching over us, that His Holy Spirit is right there in us and with us to help us in everything we do.

He wants us to know that Jesus is our Friend, and that as we walk with Him day by day good things are going to take place in our lives.

If you and I will listen to God rather than to the devil, He will cheer us up and make us feel good about ourselves. He will give us peace about the past, joy for the present and hope for the future.

Remember: The joy of the Lord is our strength and our stronghold.

Conclusion

❧

The principles that will change your life usually aren't complicated. By applying the principle of rejoicing at the onset of something that would cause you depression, your situation will change.

Part Two

—⁂—

SCRIPTURES

Scriptures to Overcome Depression

―――――――――― ❧ ――――――――――

When the righteous cry for help, the Lord hears, and delivers them out of all their distress and troubles.

Psalm 34:17

I waited patiently and expectantly for the Lord; and He inclined to me and heard my cry.

He drew me up out of a horrible pit [a pit of tumult and of destruction], out of the miry clay (froth and slime), and set my feet upon a rock, steadying my steps and establishing my goings.

And He has put a new song in my mouth, a song of praise to our God. . . .

Psalm 40:1–3

My whole being follows hard after You and clings closely to You; Your right hand upholds me.

Psalm 63:8

I wait for the Lord, I expectantly wait, and in His word do I hope.

Psalm 130:5

A gentle tongue [with its healing power] is a tree of life, but willful contrariness in it breaks down the spirit.

Proverbs 15:4

Arise [from the depression and prostration in which circumstances have kept you—rise to a new life]! Shine (be radiant with the glory of the Lord), for your light has come, and the glory of the Lord has risen upon you!

Isaiah 60:1

The Spirit of the Lord God is upon me, because the Lord has anointed and qualified me to preach the Gospel of good tidings to the meek, the poor, and afflicted; He has sent me to bind up and heal the brokenhearted, to proclaim liberty to the [physical and spiritual] captives and the opening of the prison and of the eyes to those who are bound.

To proclaim the acceptable year of the Lord [the year of His favor] and the day of vengeance of our God, to comfort all who mourn,

To grant [consolation and joy] to those who mourn in Zion—to give them an ornament (a garland or diadem) of beauty instead of ashes, the oil of joy instead of mourning, the garment [expressive] of praise instead of a heavy, burdened, and failing spirit. . . .

Isaiah 61:1–3

For God Who said, Let light shine out of darkness, has shone in our hearts so as [to beam forth] the Light for the illumination of the knowledge of the majesty and glory of God [as it is manifest in the Person and is revealed] in the face of Jesus Christ (the Messiah).

2 Corinthians 4:6

Do not fret or have any anxiety about anything, but in every circumstance and in everything, by prayer and petition (definite requests), with thanksgiving, continue to make your wants known to God.

And God's peace [shall be yours, that tranquil state of a soul assured of its salvation through Christ, and so fearing nothing from God and being content with its earthly lot of whatever sort that is, that peace] which transcends all understanding shall garrison and mount guard over your hearts and minds in Christ Jesus.

For the rest, brethren, whatever is true, whatever is worthy of reverence and is honorable and seemly, whatever is just, whatever is pure, whatever is lovely and loveable, whatever is kind and winsome and gracious, if there is any virtue and excellence, if there is anything worthy of praise, think on and weigh and take account of these things [fix your minds on them].

Philippians 4:6–8

PRAYER TO
COMBAT DEPRESSION

Father, in the name of Jesus, I come to You bearing the burden of *fatigue* my depression. It is a burden I do not need, and I leave it at Your feet now, O Lord.

Replace these downcast feelings with Your joy. Your grace is sufficient for me.

I am coming into agreement with Your Word. I need to be in Your presence. It is in You that I live and move and have my being!

Thank you!

Prayer for a Personal Relationship with the Lord

─────── ◦⟋◦ ───────

*J*esus wants to save you and fill you with the Holy Spirit more than anything. If you have never invited Jesus, the Prince of Peace, to be your Lord and Savior, I invite you to do so now. Pray the following prayer, and if you are really sincere about it, you will experience a new life in Christ.

Father,

You loved the world so much, You gave Your only begotten Son to die for our sins so that whoever believes in Him will not perish, but have eternal life.

Your Word says we are saved by grace through faith as a gift from You. There is nothing we can do to earn salvation.

I believe and confess with my mouth that Jesus Christ is Your Son, the Savior of the world. I believe He died on the cross for me and bore all of my sins, paying the price for them. I believe in my heart that You raised Jesus from the dead.

I ask You to forgive my sins. I confess Jesus as my Lord. According to Your Word, I am saved and will spend eternity with You! Thank You, Father. I am so grateful! In Jesus' name, amen.

See John 3:16; Ephesians 2:8,9; Romans 10:9,10; 1 Corinthians 15:3,4; 1 John 1:9; 4:14–16; 5:1,12,13.

ENDNOTES

---·~⌐᷉·---

Chapter 1

1. *Noah Webster's First Edition of an American Dictionary of the English Language,* (San Francisco: the Foundation for American Christian Education, 1967 and 1995 by Rosalie J. Slater. Permission to reprint the 1828 edition granted by G. & C. Merriam Company), s.v. "depression."

2. Webster, 1828 Edition, s. v. "discouraged," "discouragement."

3. *Webster's II New College Dictionary* (Boston/New York: Houghton Mifflin Company, 1995), s.v. "discourage."

4. W. E. Vine, *An Expository Dictionary of New Testament Words,* (Old Tappan, Fleming H. Revell, 1940), Vol. I, p. 300.

Chapter 2

1. James E. Strong, "Greek Dictionary of the New Testament," in *Strong's Exhaustive Concordance of the Bible* (Nashville: Abingdon, 1890), p. 77, entry #5479, s.v. "joy," Acts 20:24.

2. Strong, "Hebrew and Chaldee Dictionary," p. 37, entry #2304 from entry #2302, s.v. "joy," Nehemiah 8:10.

3. Strong, "Hebrew," p. 27, entry #1523, s.v. "joy," Habakkuk 3:18; Zephaniah 3:17.

About the Author

———— ✒️ ————

Joyce Meyer has been teaching the Word of God since 1976 and in full-time ministry since 1980. She is the bestselling author of more than sixty inspirational books, including *In Pursuit of Peace, How to Hear from God, Knowing God Intimately*, and *Battlefield of the Mind*. She has also released thousands of teaching cassettes and a complete video library. Joyce's *Enjoying Everyday Life* radio and television programs are broadcast around the world, and she travels extensively conducting conferences. Joyce and her husband, Dave, are the parents of four grown children and make their home in St. Louis, Missouri.

To contact the author write:

Joyce Meyer Ministries
P. O. Box 655
Fenton, Missouri 63026
or call: (636) 349-0303
Internet Address: www.joycemeyer.org

Please include your testimony or help received from this book when you write. Your prayer requests are welcome.

To contact the author
in Canada, please write:
Joyce Meyer Ministries Canada, Inc.
Lambeth Box 1300
London, ON N6P 1T5
or call: (636) 349-0303

In Australia, please write:
Joyce Meyer Ministries—Australia
Locked Bag 77
Mansfield Delivery Centre
Queensland 4122
or call: 07 3349 1200

In England, please write:
Joyce Meyer Ministries
P. O. Box 1549
Windsor
SL4 1GT
or call: (0) 1753-831102

Books by Joyce Meyer

Battlefield of the Kid's Mind (Spring 2006)
Approval Addiction (Spring 2005)
Ending Your Day Right
In Pursuit of Peace
The Secret Power of Speaking God's Word
Seven Things That Steal Your Joy
Starting Your Day Right
Beauty for Ashes Revised Edition
How to Hear from God
How to Hear from God Study Guide
Knowing God Intimately
The Power of Forgiveness
The Power of Determination
The Power of Being Positive
The Secrets of Spiritual Power
The Battle Belongs to the Lord
Secrets to Exceptional Living
Eight Ways to Keep the Devil Under Your Feet
Teenagers Are People Too!
Filled with the Spirit
Celebration of Simplicity
The Joy of Believing Prayer
Never Lose Heart
Being the Person God Made You to Be

Me and My Big Mouth!
Me and My Big Mouth! Study Guide
Prepare to Prosper
Do It Afraid!
Expect a Move of God in Your Life…Suddenly!
Enjoying Where You Are on the Way to
Where You Are Going
The Most Important Decision You Will Ever Make
When, God, When?
Why, God, Why?
The Word, the Name, the Blood
Battlefield of the Mind
Battlefield of the Mind Study Guide
Tell Them I Love Them
Peace
The Root of Rejection
If Not for the Grace of God
If Not for the Grace of God Study Guide

JOYCE MEYER SPANISH TITLES
Las Siete Cosas Que Te Roban el Gozo
(Seven Things That Steal Your Joy)
Empezando Tu Día Bien (Starting Your Day Right)

BY DAVE MEYER
Life Lines